SUNRISE ACRES ELEMENTARY SCHOOL
211 28th Street
Las Vegas, Nevada 89101
(702) 799-7912 Fax (702) 799-8556

How We Travel

by Rebecca Weber

Content Adviser: Allan Mueller, Engineering Specialist,
Minnesota Department of Transportation

Reading Adviser: Rosemary G. Palmer, Ph.D.,
Department of Literacy, College of Education,
Boise State University

Spyglass
BOOKS

COMPASS POINT BOOKS

Minneapolis, Minnesota

Compass Point Books
3109 West 50th Street, #115
Minneapolis, MN 55410

Visit Compass Point Books on the Internet at *www.compasspointbooks.com*
or e-mail your request to *custserv@compasspointbooks.com*

Photographs ©: Tecmap Corporation/Eric Curry/Corbis, cover; Werner Forman/Corbis, 4; Archivo
Iconografico, S.A./Corbis, 5; EyeWire, 6; Hulton/Archive by Getty Images, 7; Mark Zimmerman/Getty
Images, 8; Jiji Press/AFP/Getty Images, 9; James P. Rowan, 10; Canadian Heritage Gallery ID23259/
National Archives of Canada C-1912, 11; Corbis Sygma, 12; The U.S. Navy, 13; NASA, 14, 17, 20;
George Hall/Corbis, 15; Photo Network/Terry Brandt, 16; Bettmann/Corbis, 18; DigitalVision, 19, 21.

Creative Director: Terri Foley
Managing Editor: Catherine Neitge
Editor: Jennifer VanVoorst
Photo Researcher: Svetlana Zhurkina
Designer: Les Tranby
Educational Consultant: Diane Smolinski

Library of Congress Cataloging-in-Publication Data
Weber, Rebecca.
   How we travel / by Rebecca Weber.
      p. cm. — (Spyglass books)
   Includes bibliographical references and index.
   ISBN 0-7565-0652-2 (hardcover)
   1. Transportation—Juvenile literature. [1. Transportation.] I. Title. II. Series.
   TA1149.W43 2004
   629.04—dc22   2003024100

Contents

NOTE: Glossary words are in *bold* the first time they appear.

Before the Wheel

Long ago, people traveled by walking or by riding on animals. Then, about 6,000 years ago, the wheel was invented. Ever since then, people have searched for faster and better ways to get around.

Romans built some of the first roads more than 2,000 years ago. These roads made it easier to travel using animals or carts.

Traveling on Land

Today, most people travel on land using cars, buses, and trains. Cars, buses, and trains need *fuel* to run. These fuels are becoming hard to find. They also make the air dirty.

Cars today run on gasoline, but the very first cars were powered by steam!

Scientists are studying new ways to make these machines run. Some scientists are trying to use water as fuel for cars. Others are building cars that are powered by the sun.

Some trains don't use fuel at all. They are powered by *magnets* that push and pull the train back and forth.

Through the Water

People have traveled on water for thousands of years. Early boats floated down rivers or used sails to catch wind and use it for power.

Today, boats use mighty engines to carry people and things around the world.

The *Inuit* people hunted whales
from small boats they rowed out
into the ocean.

People also travel in the ocean using *submarines.* Some submarines travel deep enough that scientists can study the ocean floor.

Aircraft carriers are boats
that are so large, they are like
floating cities. Airplanes can
take off and land on them.

Up in the Sky

Orville and Wilbur Wright made the first airplane flight in 1903.

Today, people can travel almost any place in the world by plane.

The Wright brothers' first flight covered 120 feet (37 meters). This is about the same length as the *wingspan* of a modern airplane!

Each year, scientists find new ways for planes to be better and faster.

One new style of plane can rise straight into the air like a helicopter. Then it can fly forward like a plane.

Sound travels through the air at 750 miles (1,200 kilometers) per hour. Planes that travel faster than sound make a loud noise called a sonic boom.

Deep into Space

About 40 years ago, people started traveling into space. *Astronauts* used powerful rockets to blast off into space. Soon, astronauts were able to travel to the moon.

In 1969, Neil Armstrong became the first person to walk on the moon.

In 1981, people began using the *space shuttle* to travel in space. The space shuttle could blast off like a rocket and land like an airplane.

Today, scientists are looking for ways to send people deeper into space. How do you think they will travel there?

Glossary

astronauts–people who travel in space

fuel–something that is used as a source of power, such as coal, wood, or gasoline

Inuit–the people who have lived in northern North America for more than 1,000 years

magnets–objects that can make pieces of iron or steel move without touching them

Romans–people who lived in ancient Rome

scientists–people who work to solve problems and learn about the world

space shuttle–a spacecraft that carries people into space and back to Earth

submarines–ships that can travel underwater

wingspan–the distance between the tips of an aircraft's wings

Learn More

Books

Armentrout, David and Patricia. *Planes.* Vero
Beach, Fla.: Rourke Publishing, 2004.

Ring, Susan. *From Here to There.* Bloomington,
Minn.: Yellow Umbrella Books, 2004.

On the Web

For more information on **How We Travel,** use
FactHound to track down Web sites related
to this book.

1. Go to ***www.facthound.com***
2. Type in a search word related
to this book or this book ID:
0756506522.
3. Click on the **Fetch It** button.

Your trusty FactHound will fetch
the best Web sites for you!

Index

GR: K
Word Count: 266

From Rebecca Weber

Whenever I travel to a new place, I enjoy learning about people and their daily lives. I hope this book opens up a little bit of the world for you!

24